I Love Sports

Tae Kwon Do

by Cari Meister

Bullfrog Books

Ideas for Parents and Teachers

Bullfrog Books let children practice reading informational text at the earliest reading levels. Repetition, familiar words, and photo labels support early readers.

Before Reading

- Discuss the cover photo. What does it tell them?
- Look at the picture glossary together. Read and discuss the words.

Read the Book

- "Walk" through the book and look at the photos. Let the child ask questions. Point out the photo labels.
- Read the book to the child, or have him or her read independently.

After Reading

- Prompt the child to think more. Ask: Have you ever done tae kwon do? Have you watched a match? What does each person do?

Bullfrog Books are published by Jump!
5357 Penn Avenue South
Minneapolis, MN 55419
www.jumplibrary.com

Library of Congress Cataloging-in-Publication Data

Names: Meister, Cari.
Title: Tae Kwon Do / by Cari Meister.
Description: Minneapolis, MN: Jump!, Inc. [2017] © 2017. | Series: Bullfrog Books. I Love Sports Includes index. | Audience: Ages: 5–8. Audience: Grades: K to Grade 3.
Identifiers: LCCN 2016008095
ISBN 9781620313633 (hard cover: alk. paper)
ISBN 9781624964107 (e-book)
Subjects: LCSH: Tae kwon do—Juvenile literature.
Classification: LCC GV1114.9 .M35 2016
DDC 796.815/7—dc23
LC record available at http://lccn.loc.gov/2016008095

Editor: Kirsten Chang
Series Designer: Ellen Huber
Book Designer: Molly Ballanger
Photo Researcher: Molly Ballanger

Photo Credits: All photos by Shutterstock except: Alamy, 14–15; Getty, 20–21; iStock, 13, 19; Thinkstock, 3, 4, 5, 23tl; Vladimir57/Shutterstock.com, 14–15, 16–17, 18, 23bl, 23br.

Printed in the United States of America at Corporate Graphics in North Mankato, Minnesota.

Table of Contents

Let's Spar!

Put on a dobok.

Tie your belt.

Let's spar!

Leo warms up.

He stretches.

He kicks.

Hwan is a sabum.
It means "master."
He teaches Leo
how to block.

He shows Leo how
to kick and punch.

Today is a match.

Sam and Jo will spar.

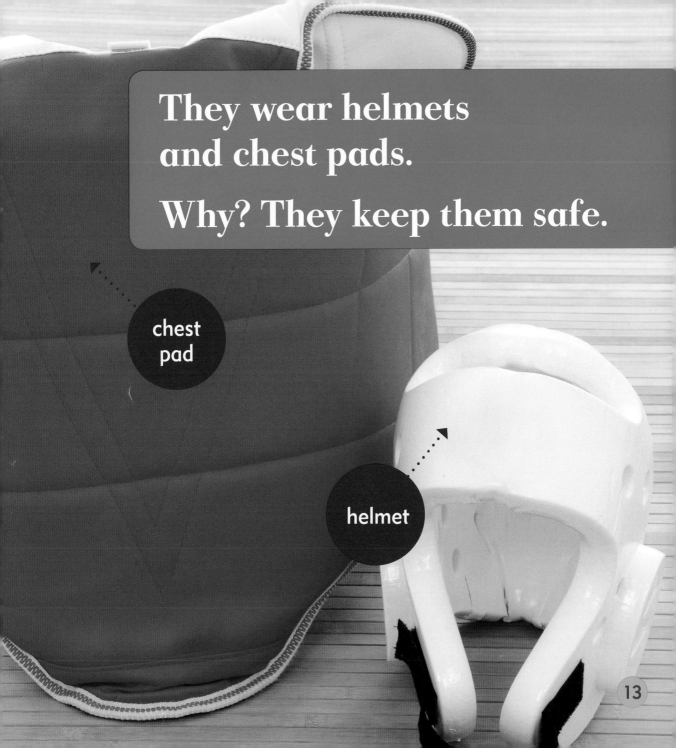

They wear helmets
and chest pads.

Why? They keep them safe.

chest
pad

helmet

13

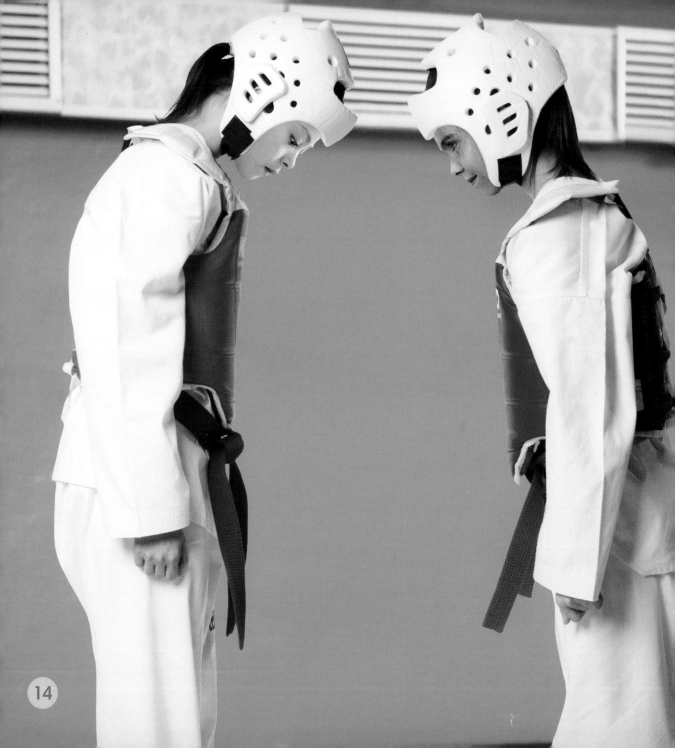

The girls meet
on the mat.

They bow.

Sam kicks.

She hits Jo's chest.

Sam gets one point.

Jo does a roundhouse kick.
Wow! It hits Sam's helmet.

Jo gets three points.
The girl with the
most points wins.

19

Want to try?

Put on your pads.

Kick! Block!

Tae kwon do is fun.

Sparring Gear

dobok
The name of the tae kwon do uniform comes from the Korean words *do*, meaning "way," and *bok*, meaning clothing.

chest pad
Called a *hogu*, a chest protector should cover both the chest and the shoulders.

belt
Called a *tti*, a student's belt color shows his or her level of skill and understanding.

helmet
Called a *homyun*, this soft helmet protects the head and ears from hits and kicks.

Picture Glossary

dobok
The white pants and jacket used for tae kwon do.

sabum
A tae kwon do teacher; it means "master" in Korean.

roundhouse kick
When you spin and then kick.

spar
To fight.

Index

To Learn More

Learning more is as easy as 1, 2, 3.

1) Go to www.factsurfer.com

2) Enter "taekwondo" into the search box.

3) Click the "Surf" button to see a list of websites.

With factsurfer.com, finding more information is just a click away.